APPLYING HAND BRAKE

A TEENAGE BOY'S HONEST ACCOUNT ABOUT GOD AND PORN.

BY BEN DYER

 **RESOURCES**

ISBN 978-1-905691-57-9

A CIP catalogue record for this book is available from the British Library

First published in 2018 by Naked Truth Resources, an imprint of:

McKnight & Bishop Ltd. | 26 Walworth Crescent, Darlington, DL3 0TX

http://www.mcknightbishop.com | info@mcknightbishop.com

This book has been typeset in Avenir and *Handbrake*

* Custom font created by Hannah Wheeler | @hannahwheelerillustration

Cover Design by Hannah Wheeler
Edited by André Adefope

Printed and bound in Great Britain by Cloc Ltd.

The paper used in this book has been made from wood independently certified as having come from sustainable forests.

Acknowledgements

Writing a book is a long process! And there are a few people I would like to thank.

Firstly, I want to thank Jesus. I know this sounds cheesy, but without him I'm nothing.

I want to thank my wife Bethany for supporting and encouraging me and helping me to discover real love.

I also want to thank all the people that made this book possible. James Lawrence for encouraging me to write it and spending hours reading over the first drafts. Ian Henderson for taking a risk on it. André Adefope for his patience reading, re-reading and re-re-reading it while editing it. And Bethany MacDonald for her valuable input. Without your help and encouragement this book would not exist.

Contents

Endorsements

"Very honest and helps equip you against future struggles."

11 year old lad

"The book is the perfect mix of honest and relatable experiences, real truth about God's views, and amazing advice on how to live as a Christian in the modern world."

15 year old lad

"Applying the Handbrake is one of the best books I have read on this incredibly relevant topic. It's packed full of descriptive personal experience, fabulous metaphors, practical application and profound Biblical truth. I laughed, empathised and was inspired. If you struggle in this area this book will give you a reassurance of God's heart for you, a companion on the journey and strategies to break free. I wholeheartedly recommend it."

Phil Knox, Head of Mission to Young Adults, Evangelical Alliance

"If I'd read this book when I was a teenager I would've found it so encouraging and genuinely helpful as I fought similar battles over the years."

Tim Funnell, Project Manager of LiNX Christian Youth Trust

"Applying the Handbrake is an honest and humorous account of a real life struggle with masturbation and porn – this is such a common issue in our 21st century society yet few want to admit it or talk about it. Ben brings the problem out into the open brilliantly with his own story. It's straight to the point, funny, concise, easy to read – I simply couldn't put it down! It's a great book for teenage lads, for all experiencing similar struggles, and for all those working with adolescents."

Andy Milne, Leader of Sorted Youth Church, Bradford

Foreword

I run a charity that talks about pornography, ALOT. We're passionate about helping people understand the damaging impact it can have, and helping people who are already feeling battered and broken by porn's punches.

Porn ruins lives. Every day I see the damage it causes young and old, male and female. The people behind the screen, mostly women, being exploited and even abused to provide fresh content for the millions of daily clicks. Then there are guys and girls who get caught up in a trap of dependency. There are literally millions of stories to tell, and we want to tell as many as we can. That's why I was excited when Ben approached us with HIS story.

Ben's story involves being a teenage lad who was struggling and didn't know who to talk to. Not enough people were answering the many questions he, and many young lads like him, have about porn, masturbation, sex, relationships, lust and life. Throw God and faith into the mix, and the confusion, guilt, and misunderstanding seems to get bigger and the number of people offering help and practical advice gets smaller.

It's our hope that this book and Ben's story will start to change that.

Ben has written a book which cuts through all of the haze, unanswered questions and concerns. He never pretends to be perfect, and he honestly shares his mistakes, weaknesses and regrets in a real and relatable way, while giving straight-forward practical advice which anyone can put into action. He clearly outlines biblical teaching on sex, masturbation and God's desire for our relationships, while wrapping it from top to bottom in grace, second chances, and God's love for us.

It's short, easy to understand, filled with humour, non-judg-mental advice, and gets straight to the point.

This is a very personal story, and highlights Ben's unique per-spective as a Christian teenage boy. I believe, alongside oth-ers, it's a story that needs to be told. If you happen to be a (Christian) teenage lad, I think you will love this and relate to it. If you're not, without question, you'll still find some practical advice and also get a glimpse into the mind of teenage boys! (You have been warned.)

Ian Henderson

CEO and Founder of the Naked Truth Project

Preface

When I was 19 I can remember telling my pastor that one day I was going to write a book about porn and masturbation. As a teenager I struggled with porn, masturbation, lust, and generally everything else that involved the female species (including talking to them). In that time, I never met anyone, read anything, or heard anything that really helped me in my struggle. So for years I battled it alone, feeling guilty and ashamed. I tried to read some books about 'guy stuff' hoping that one of them would help, but I never connected with any of them. And so, much to my surprise (and I suspect my English teacher's surprise), I wrote this book.

My hope and prayer is that this book will help you. I've been completely honest (and I'm hoping my parents never read this…) about my struggle and what I've learnt along the way. My life isn't perfect and I don't have all the answers, but I'm convinced that the more we talk about this, the more we can help each other. That's why at the end of each chapter there are some questions to think about, and ideally chat about with others.

Through my life, I have discovered a God who is bigger than my mess, stronger than my weakness, and more loving than I deserve. I hope and pray that this book will help you discover that too.

Am I Weird Or Normal?

We all watch porn, it's normal, right? It's just a bit of harmless entertainment, people in the films are having a good time, we all enjoy watching it, it's natural, so let's just get on with it.

So what if I said I was a Christian? Would that make it a bit weird? Going to church in the morning and then going home to watch porn on my phone? Some people think Christians shouldn't be watching porn and shouldn't be masturbating, but other Christians think it's harmless, so we shouldn't worry, stress or feel guilty about it.

So, which one is it?

Your body wants you to watch it; and your friends say porn and masturbation is okay and make jokes about it, but it's not something you post as your status: 'Just watched some porn #feelgreat.' Films show us it's normal, but some parents disagree. Some experts say porn doesn't portray real loving sex and that it forces the actresses to participate. Some say masturbation is simply part of growing up, others say you will go blind. So is it okay or not?

· ● ● ·●●●● ●●━●●· ●

The Changing Room

My story, and my confusion, began when I was five years old.

I can remember the first time I saw them. I had gone swimming with my mum and sister, and like all five-year-old boys, I had no option but to get changed in the ladies changing room. While I was quietly keeping my head down, trying to be discrete about the fact I had a penis, a woman quickly walked across into our changing room section from the showers. The woman was about 30 years old, with long brown hair and a slim physique. She got her clothes out of the locker and it was then that it happened.

She dropped her towel and before my eyes were a big pair of boobs.

I hadn't ever seen boobs before on any non-family woman and was immediately fascinated. I stared straight at them and it seemed like time stood still, all my worries about swimming went away. I don't know how long I stared for, but it must have been longer than socially acceptable, because the woman looked at me and quietly asked me, "Are you OK?" I shyly murmured an answer and rushed out of the changing rooms. This was my first encounter, and even at five years old I was fascinated.

Even back then, staring at that woman I would have called myself a Christian. In fact, I cannot remember a time I wasn't a Christian. My parents were both Christians and every week I would go to Sunday school and make paper sheep or pretend to be the animals going into the ark. The problem was that being a Christian didn't seem like it would complement the other fascination in my life – boobs. In reality, much of my life has been dominated by a struggle between Jesus and boobs.

ᴡᴡᴡᴡᴡᴡᴡᴡ

Auditioning The Finger Puppet

I first masturbated at 12 years old, and I can remember it well. It was the middle of the day and I was standing in the middle of my bedroom – very bizarre. I didn't masturbate because I was horny or I had a picture in front of me. I masturbated because I was curious.

From the age of about ten I had known about this thing called masturbation, although I was a bit unsure of the details. I had thought that if you played with your balls a bit then something good happened. People called it 'wanking', 'jerking off', 'touching yourself', 'auditioning the finger puppet', 'taking the sausage hostage', or 'applying the handbrake'. I had tried this a few times, but nothing had happened so I had given up. But when I was 12 a whole new world was opened up to me. A boy called Chris from school had insulted another boy and called him a 'wanker', while imitating the action towards him. I realised from his imitation of masturbating that if I tried that on my balls they would probably become detached from my body. It dawned on me, you don't play with your balls, but your penis!

I remember the feeling of masturbating, like nothing else I had ever felt, and I didn't know if I liked it or if I didn't. Needless to say, after about a week I decided that I would try it again, since everyone at school talked about it like it was good and enjoyable. Slowly, but surely, I began to slip into the pattern of masturbating and it became part of my life.

At first I can't remember thinking about anything while masturbating; it was more just trying to figure out this totally alien experience. This quickly changed as I began taking more of an interest in the female species. By the time I was 13 I was masturbating frequently and looking at pictures of women. These pictures began with women in underwear or bikinis, but over time the women would be wearing fewer clothes and becoming more active.

I felt bad about it, I thought I may be weird, but I couldn't stop.

I think every Christian, and probably most people, deep down feels guilty about masturbating and looking at porn, there's something that doesn't feel quite right about it. I would feel guilty afterwards and tell myself to stop, but from

13 years old I would masturbate, day after day. It became normal.

My first experience with a real, breathing girl happened at the age of 14. I was quite a shy kid, so while a lot of my friends had kissed a real girl, I hadn't. I say real because I had practised on Barbies and the back of my hand to perfect my technique (I don't think it worked). This is where my experience with girls got weird. I had oral sex before I had my first kiss. That is pretty odd in anybody's world, but at the age of 14 I was looking at porn so much that oral sex had become normal in my mind. The guilt I felt afterwards was unbelievable – like nothing I had ever felt before. Deep down I knew what happened wasn't right and I felt that I was a disappointment to myself and to God. I vowed to never touch my penis again. I vowed to never look at porn again. I vowed to sort my life out.

The feelings of guilt and my passionate vows worked for a while. I felt so bad about what I had done; I was determined to never touch myself again, but it didn't take me long to fall back into old habits and; before I knew it I was looking at porn and masturbating nearly every day. I couldn't escape; my whole world would revolve around when I would next be able to masturbate. It's all I would think about during the day, and I felt trapped in a cycle of messing up and feeling guilty about it, but then doing it and enjoying it, then feeling bad again. I wasn't sure if everyone felt like this, or if it was just me.

Sick Of The Cycle

Until I was nearly 18, this was my life. A life filled with guilt. A life dominated by my relationship to my penis. It wasn't enjoyable. I wanted to stop, but I couldn't. My feelings towards myself and God were determined by whether I'd masturbated that day or not. I felt hopeless and there seemed no way out.

When I was 18 things changed slightly.

A few different things happened at the same time. I reached a point in my life where I was sick of the cycle of messing up, feeling guilty, messing up, feeling guilty. It was also at this time that I began to spend time with God on a daily basis rather than whenever I just felt like it.

Another big step in my journey happened when I told people about my problem. I went on a Christian gap year and we did an activity about our past. I told everyone that I felt addicted to masturbating and looking at porn. I had never told anyone before and there I was telling a group of people, but it lifted an incredible weight off my shoulders, and I began to feel slightly free.

I could end it there. I could tell you I'm married now and it's all okay, and pretend that marriage is the cure to sexual struggles. I could tell you that I have an amazing wife and I masturbated for the last time about one week before my wedding. But it's not that simple. I had to understand why I felt guilty. I had to realise that God could help me in this struggle. I had to learn to help myself. I had to learn what good sex was and the lies that pornography had taught me. I had to know what was weird and what was 'normal'.

I'm not sorted in the slightest, I get things wrong all the time and I mess up. I regret some of the things I did and regret the times I failed, but I have hope. I want to share my whole story with you. Not just the 'happy ending', not just the 'exciting' bits, not just the guilt, not just the hope, but all of it.

The God bit, the porn bit, the masturbation bit.

I want you to hear about what I learned. And I want you to know that there is a life free from being addicted to porn and masturbation. There is a life free from compulsive sexual desire. We don't need to be controlled by it, or be dominated by the times we mess up and walk away from God. Life is found with hard-work, courage, and above all, life is found in Jesus. You will have to fight, it won't be easy, but you can be free from a life controlled by your penis.

— · — · — · —

STOP AND REFLECT

Ask yourself:

- When did you first see porn?

- How often do you watch porn/masturbate?

- Do you think it's a problem in your life?

Exercise

- Circle words that define how you feel after reading this chapter:

normal, weird, embarrassed, relieved, excited, confused, unholy, hopeful, uncomfortable, better, relaxed, happy, sad, good, worried, interested, bad, other:

Stop and Reflect With Others

- What was your first experience of porn?

- Chat about one or two of the words you circled and why.

"Sex-Ed"

It had seemed like a good idea at the time, but as I stood up and began to speak I had doubts. The day was 12th September 2009 and I will always remember that date because it was the day I got married. We had 100 family and friends packed into a small, ancient barn outside York and I had just stood up to deliver my speech.

Unfortunately, for everyone else in the room, I have an awkward sense of humour. Not that my sense of humour is awkward (although many people think it is), but I find awkward situations funny. Everyone can remember a situation when someone says something and the whole room goes completely silent in shock. Well it's those sorts of situations that I find hilarious. This sense of humour generally gets me in trouble, as I try to create those awkward-you-could-hear-a-pin-drop moments.

Well I decided that in my wedding speech I would create one of those awkward-pin-drop moments. And not just for a couple of seconds, but for the majority of my speech.

Two weeks before the wedding I had been on holiday with my family and after a few glasses of wine the conversation turned to 'the wedding night'. In a jokey way my dad asked, "do you know what you're doing?" I replied confidently, "of course I do, you just wiggle a bit". My dad laughed, while my mum looked shocked and concerned. My mum softly asked, "do you actually know what you're doing? You can't just wiggle. I think we need to share some advice".

I think my mum actually thought I was going to "just wiggle a bit" and so the family sat around and proceeded to give me 20 sex tips. At one point my sister (who is a doctor) actually drew a diagram of the female 'area' because she was worried I might get it wrong.

As I stood up to give my speech I thanked everyone for coming and then launched straight into the bulk of the speech. "Sex tip number 1: Don't wiggle. Sex tip number 2: Shower first, no skank. Sex tip number 3: ... etc." Yes, I did read out 20 sex tips for most of my wedding speech. Yes, the person directly in my line of vision for the whole speech was my wife's granddad.

Yes, it was awkward. But my education started long before this speech and conversation with my family.

000000000000

Learning Outside The Classroom

In the UK, everyone who goes to school has to have sex education classes. These classes are supposed to teach you about sex. I had my first class at 14, at which point I had probably discovered, been told about, or seen most things a human could see regarding sex. In the class we were shown a video of a man dressed up as a sperm running around trying to fertilise an egg. Needless to say that like most people, I didn't learn anything about sex, love, or relationships from these sex education classes.

Another normally amusing way that people are educated about sex is the dreaded talk with a parent; mine was with my dad. Some of you may have horror stories but all I remember is my dad had a talk with my brother and I when I was about 9.

The church that I went to was silent on the issue. They were either very naïve and thought no church boy would ever struggle to control their hormones, or it was the elephant in the room and treated like Lord Voldemort, the big issue no one dare mention or talk about.

Instead, I learned about the birds and the bees through our culture. Friends would tell outrageous stories of how they had sex with 213 women in one night. Films taught me what was right and wrong and how relationships should work. I learnt the nitty gritty, practical details of sex through porn. From a young age, I was being taught what was right and wrong, good and bad, normal and abnormal, acceptable and unacceptable through these films, TV shows, porn, social media posts, friends, music and the fantasies of a teenage boy. I, like so many other people, was left to be educated by culture, and it certainly taught me something.

From an early age culture taught me:

- Sex and sexual activity is fun and should be enjoyed freely without guilt or shame.

- It's therefore normal and healthy to watch porn and masturbate.

- Sleeping around is fun.

- Sex should be a part of every relationship.

- The more people you have sex with, the more of a man you are.

- If you can get a woman to act like a porn star in bed you get extra man points.

The list could go on.

Our culture continually tells us these messages. Friends brag about their conquests with women. Films show us that 'real men' have sex with lots of women. Newspapers tell stories of threesomes. Social media shows us pictures of semi-naked women. Advertisements tell us that if we buy their products we will get the girls. Radio shows insist that so long as you love each other, sex is natural. Porn shows men how to have sex. Musicians sing boastfully about one-night-stands.

Now I realise that our culture lies. None of these things ever made me happy or satisfied. This is a problem because most of us believe this lie, live this lie, and then realise far too late (if ever at all) that we've been lied to.

I believed the lie. I believed that porn, masturbation, touching girls, sex and everything else was normal, good, and always right. I believed that it would make me happy and provide satisfaction. I lived the lie, but porn has never made me happy; in fact, it made me miserable. Masturbation never gave me satisfaction; it made me constantly unsatisfied. Touching girls never gave meaning to my life; it took meaning away. But because I wanted to do these things, and I had been educated that they were normal, I dived straight in.

I was being influenced, pressured, and educated outside of the classroom by our culture, like most of us are. We spend little time listening to any other voices. In a standard week, I would expect to hear ten times as many messages that "sex is about having fun", or, "stare at good looking people, that's why they're there", than I would hearing things like, "people's bodies are not something that can simply be used and abused to turn you on", or "porn won't make you happy", or "that's a human being, someone's sister or daughter".

Without any other voices in the world telling me the truth, I believed the lie.

Good Sex

I think one of the reasons why it's so easy to believe the sex education our culture teaches us is because often it's so near the truth. Sex is good. Being intimate is good. God created a world and as part of that he created sex. He didn't have to. He could have created a world where we reproduce like other animals where sex doesn't happen, but He didn't.

In the Garden of Eden, God commands Adam and Eve to have sex. He says to them, "Be fruitful and increase in number; fill the earth and subdue it."[1]

In other words, "Adam and Eve: go and have sex." There's even a whole book of the Bible that's a celebration of love, intimacy, and sex called Song of Solomon. Just listen to this: "Let him kiss me with the kisses of his mouth … Take me away with you – let us hurry! Let the king bring me into his chambers."[2] The Bible speaks of a God who wants us to enjoy sex, but the Bible also speaks of a God who cares about us and doesn't want to see us hurt, empty, dissatisfied,

---

1   Genesis 1:28
2   Song of Songs 1:2-4

trapped, addicted and unfulfilled; where we are treating women as objects instead of human beings.

Because God created sex and made it and everything surrounding it to be so powerful, it can also be dangerous and damaging when misused. And so before Adam and Eve had sex, which happened when the Bible says they became one flesh, God placed a boundary around it: marriage. Adam and Eve respected each other, made vows and promises before God and made a commitment to each other.[3] God didn't design sex to happen after marriage to spoil our fun, but to stop us getting hurt and feeling empty, dissatisfied, trapped, addicted and unfulfilled.

I remember when I was younger my uncle gave us all the James Bond films. One summer holiday my brother and I watched every single one of them. I loved the car chase scenes. I remember watching them and thinking, 'I can't wait to start driving' because it looked so exciting. But those car chase scenes aren't real; they unhelpfully make driving look like it's pure excitement. Real driving isn't like that.

Porn isn't like real sex either.

3   Genesis 2:22-24

32

Porn is designed to entertain. But real sex is different; it's not just an exciting chase scene and it's more than a momentary thrill. Our sex education needs to be about real sex because if we just chase entertainment, then real life will seem boring and unfulfilling. Porn leads us into a world of fake sex which I found hurtful, unfulfilling, disconnecting, and selfish. But the truth is that real sex within God's boundaries is amazing, fulfilling, uniting and selfless.

Sex Is Everywhere, But That's Not New

I used to think that this obsession our culture has with sex was a new thing. That the rise in pornography has led to a society obsessed with sex, but this obsession is nothing new.

The idea that our current Western culture is more driven by sex than any other before is simply wrong. Societies and cultures throughout the world were, are, and will continue to be driven by sex. For example, the ancient Greeks celebrated sex, sexual desires and the phallus (penis). In the temple of Aphrodite the altar was lined with model penises. The role models of Greek society, the gods, were having sex all the time. In Roman culture the annual Bacchanalian festival gave Romans the chance to have lots of sex with lots of people, until it was finally outlawed in 186BC.

During the Medieval period nothing changed, sex continued to play a major part in society. Prostitution was common. In the seventh century Alcuin of York said, "The land has been absolutely submerged under a flood of [premarital sex], adultery and incest, so that the very semblance of modesty is entirely absent." And even in Victorian London some estimated that there were as many as 80,000 prostitutes serving a population of 2 million.[4]

From the beginning of time, societies around the world have been obsessed with sex and everything that surrounds it. We need to learn that as humans, we are obsessed with sex like many others before us.

I often like to think, 'I'm a Christian, so I don't think the way that our culture does. Our sexualised culture isn't a reflection of me.' But honestly, I've been affected. I'm still affected by it. A part of me does believe that sex and sexual activity is

---

4   p476 Mayhew, H. (1985) London Labour and the London Poor. London: Penguin.

simply fun and has no consequences. Some part of me does think that 'real men' have sex with lots of women. Some part of me agrees with everything our culture says about sex. Some part of me still wants to believe the lies.

I realised that what I needed was to learn about the truth and learn about real sex. This is the kind of sex God speaks about and we read in the Bible, the kind of sex that brings joy and fulfilment rather than emptiness and disappointment. This is the type of sex which respects the person I'm with. I needed to stop listening to the bad education and lies that my culture was feeding me.

Lies, Lies And More Lies

It may seem obvious, but to change my mindset the first thing I had to do was stop listening to these lies and stop learning from my bad education. For too long I had believed, wished and wanted the lies to be true and ignored the truth. I wonder how much time we spend listening to these lies and how much time we spend hearing truth?

If you in any way struggle with porn, masturbation, sex, or anything surrounding it, then listening to our culture of lies will make your struggles more difficult. That isn't to say you should go and live in a cave, but it is to say that many of us have the balance way out. We're constantly bombarded with lies and rarely hear any truth. We rarely read the Bible, rarely pray, rarely talk to our friends about anything that is slightly embarrassing or shameful because it's so much easier to spend hours every day watching TV, checking social media, playing computer games, taking the perfect selfie, talking to our friends about sex, trying to have sex, watching porn, masturbating and dreaming about hot women.

However much we try, we will become whatever we listen to. We will accept as 'truth' whatever floods our mind the most. We will live a life that reflects whatever influences us the most. And the sad thing is that for many of us (including myself) the thing that influences us the most is the culture we live in: the sex driven, truth destroying, entrapping context we live in. The powerful message of our culture often drowns out the saving message of Jesus.

Now I'm not an 'anti-world' Christian. Some bits of culture are amazing, and God created and loves the world, but on the issue of sex and fulfilment, it robbed me of the truth. Sadly, if pastors, fathers, mothers, youth workers, brothers, sisters, school teachers or friends don't teach a person about good sex and relationships, our culture will teach us its version.

We will never find freedom and truth if we continue to listen and accept what our culture is saying. We will never overcome our struggles if our culture is the most influential, important, and valuable influence in our life. The first thing we need to do is realise that, for most of us, our education is incomplete. We need to hear more about real sex and good sex rather than unreal pornographic sex which feeds us lies. We need to turn down the volume on the bad education.

Stop and Reflect

- What is your definition of porn?

The definition I use is: Anything designed to stimulate sexual excitement. If this is true, would music videos be porn? Would Fifty Shades of Grey be porn? What else do you see or hear that could be porn?

Stop and Reflect With Others

- Who gave you the sex talk and how was it?

- Talk about why you listed some of the things that could be called 'porn' using the definition above.

- Do you think porn and/or masturbation can ever be good?

Campsite Confusion

Have you ever tried to get some information but been more confused as a result?

I've lived up North all my life, I've never lived in London, I don't go to London very often and I have no idea where anything is. On the rare occasions that I go I normally end up having to get the Tube. I find the Tube incredibly confusing. I look at the Underground map, I check what Google says, I ask people who live in London and most of the time they all give me different and complicated answers. I check the internet and it says, 'Take the Northern line to Bank Station, then walk to Monument Underground and get on the District line to Blackfriars.' However, when I ask a friend, they put on their 'I'm-an-expert' voice and explain to me, "This might be delayed today so you should take the Circle line, Metropolitan line, or Hammersmith line to Farringdon station and then take the Thameslink to Blackfriars." The Tube always confuses me and the more information I ask for, the more confused I become.

I felt the same confusion when it came to porn and masturbation. I think part of me always felt it was wrong, but another part of me believed the lie our culture teaches us. This confusion was increased by Christians around me. When I was 14, I went to a Christian festival for a week. It was the kind of festival where you camp and go to talks and worship services all day everyday. At this time I had successfully worked out how to masturbate and naked women were constantly on my mind. I went to a seminar, especially for teenagers about 'man-stuff' (another way of saying anything related to sex). I was looking forward to it as I had barely heard anything from a Christian perspective on masturbation or porn, and this was something I was really struggling with.

After the seminar had finished I left more confused than when I started.

Apparently masturbation wasn't wrong by itself. Masturbation was better than having sex with your girlfriend, so if you knew you might have sex, you should just masturbate instead. Does that make masturbation okay? Is that really going to stop any horny young boy from having sex? For the next few months, I justified masturbation as being okay, since a Christian man who speaks at the front had told me that it was.

Some of us may have similar stories. 'I read in a book that masturbation is good for you,' or, 'A Christian friend told me that watching porn is simply enjoying God's creation.' Confusion, confusion, and more confusion.

Many people who read the Bible will think some of their thoughts and actions about sex are wrong, not because sex is wrong, but because they are using people in their fantasies and on their screens to gain sexual satisfaction. Their conscience tell them this isn't right. For most of us we don't need to be told what we are doing, looking at, or fantasising about is wrong. We know it all too well. We feel the shame of it daily. And we live under it all the time.

But we must take away the confusion. We cannot just stay camped in a place which raises more questions than answers. We need to be clear about what's right and wrong so we can escape the place we are trapped in.

Jesus' disciples wouldn't have been left confused after Jesus taught them what was expected of them. In Matthew 5:27-30 Jesus says:

"You have heard that it was said, 'You shall not commit adultery.' But I tell you that anyone who looks at a woman lustfully has already committed adultery with her in his heart. If your right eye causes you to stumble, gouge it out and throw it away. It is better for you to lose one part of your body than for your whole body to be thrown into hell. And if your right hand causes you to stumble, cut it off and throw it away. It is better for you to lose one part of your body than for your whole body to go into hell."

In Jewish society adultery was regarded as a serious wrong doing. It's the seventh commandment[5] and the punishment for adultery would be death.[6] In the ancient world adultery was known as 'the great sin.' If a married or betrothed woman was to sleep with any man other than her husband, they could both be killed.

---

5   Exodus 20:14, Deuteronomy 5:18
6   Leviticus 20:10, Deuteronomy 22:22

Adultery, however, always involved a physical action. It involved having sexual contact with a married man or a married woman. You couldn't legally be killed for staring at a woman. Even though there were no punishments for lust, Jews would have accepted lustful looks and thoughts as wrong. Before Jesus had even been born it had been written, 'For the person with a mind that is pure with love does not look on a woman for the purpose of having sexual relations'.[7] But the Jewish people had never linked a look with adultery.

For Jesus, it's not just what happens on the outside that's important, but what happens on the inside. He doesn't just focus on what we do, but also on what we look at, think about, desire and feel. He says that people who 'look' at a woman have committed adultery. People who 'look' at a woman and just see her as an object (and when women do it to men too) have committed one of the most serious wrong doings. People who 'look' at a woman have committed 'the great sin'.

Some may think, 'I look at women every day! Does this mean Jesus wants me to walk around with a blindfold on?' Well thankfully not. Jesus isn't saying you cannot look at women.

---

7   The Testament of Benjamin 8:2

Jesus isn't even saying you cannot look at a woman and think she's attractive. Jesus says adultery is when we look at a woman (other than your wife) and want to have sex with her. Adultery is when we look at a woman and imagine her naked. Adultery is when we look at a woman and get a stirring in our loins and make it all about 'my needs' and don't respect her as a person. Adultery is when we masturbate and sexually fantasise about a woman. Adultery is when we watch porn.

Now before you start to feel too bad, we need to remember that although Jesus gives us some tough commands, he also gives more grace than we could imagine. There is a story in the Bible of a famous king called David and his adulterous relationship with Bathsheba. One evening David sees Bathsheba having a bath on her roof. The Bible describes Bathsheba as 'very beautiful',[8] but married to a solider in David's army. As David keeps looking at this woman his penis begins to do all the thinking, so David invites her over, sleeps with her, and sends her husband to his death. David doesn't even realise (or care that) he has done anything wrong until a prophet called Nathan visits him and shows him his sin. "Then David confessed to Nathan, 'I've sinned against the

---

8   2 Samuel 11:2

Lord.' Nathan replied, 'Yes, but the Lord has forgiven you, and you won't die for this sin.'"[9]

The clear and tough way Jesus describes adultery is hard for us to live up to, but we follow a God who is kind, merciful, and forgiving. David knew he had messed up, yet the first words God speaks through his prophet to David are that He forgives David's sin. When we understand that we have messed up, the first words God speak to us are, "I forgive you." Jesus doesn't walk ahead of us waiting for us to catch up, Jesus walks beside us, carrying us, holding our hand and picking us up when we fall down.

•—•—•—•—•—•—••••••••—•—•—•—

Redrawing My Boundaries

The principle that Jesus laid out in Matthew 5 on lust has a danger of being under-applied or over-applied. We all draw boundaries of what we think is acceptable and what we think is wrong, in all areas of our lives. For example, I think it's acceptable to watch cat videos on YouTube for ten minutes per day, while I think it's wrong to watch cat videos for 22 hours a day.

---

9   2 Samuel 12:13 NLT

These ideas about right and wrong are informed by lots of factors, such as our upbringing or our personality, but a very important factor is the culture we live in. The Western world largely accepts drinking alcohol, but some cultures think any amount of drinking is wrong.

But when it comes to sex, where should the boundaries be? Can I masturbate? Can I watch porn?

///////////////

More Straight Talking: Masturbation

This often seems so confusing. So, is it right or wrong?

The Bible doesn't give a straight answer to this question. No verse talks about masturbation directly. But I'm going to tell you what I wish that person had told me when I was 14 at that Christian camp: I think masturbation is wrong. God wants the best for us and even if we masturbate 10,000 times God will forgive us, but masturbation is not part of God's good plan for sex.

I think masturbation is wrong for three reasons: the thoughts that go with it, the slippery slope to dependency, and because it's not real sex.

Firstly, I have heard about people being able to masturbate without thinking about anything sexual and maybe that is true for some people. However, for me masturbation was always linked to me either looking at or thinking about sex. I remember attempting to masturbate with a clear mind, but as soon as I got turned on my mind instantly started drifting to thinking about hot women and sex no matter how much I tried. For most people, we cannot masturbate without looking at or thinking about women or sex. Most teenagers now look at porn before or while masturbating too, and it becomes part of their thoughts. Jesus was very clear that our thoughts matter.

Secondly, I think masturbation is wrong because it can lead to people feeling addicted and is a slippery slope into a life ruled by your penis. My difficult journey didn't start with porn. My journey into a world I couldn't escape started with masturbation. It was masturbation that led me to watching porn, not the other way around. As I got deeper into this world both porn and masturbation ended up supporting each other and driving me further into the darkness. For some of you it may have started the other way round, but they both end up feeding off each other. It becomes almost impossible to ignore and we can feel trapped and dependent on it. This isn't what God wants for us.

Lastly, masturbation isn't real sex. God created sex to be a team effort and not a solo mission. Real sex at its heart is selfless, it's not about me but rather it's about the other person. Whereas masturbation at its heart is selfish, it's all about me me me. In Genesis 2:24 it says, 'That is why a man leaves his father and mother and is united to his wife, and they become one flesh'. It doesn't say, 'That is why a man locks himself in his room and is united to his penis.' Real sex is a joining together of two bodies, hearts and souls in love, commitment and unity, with mutual sexual attraction. Masturbation is just a cheap imitation that falls outside of the world God created.

God wants us to be happy, He wants us to enjoy sex and be satisfied. I think masturbation is wrong because it ultimately robs us of the person God created us to be. Whether you struggle with masturbation or you don't, you are always accepted and wanted by God, but we need to reduce the confusion.

△△△△△△△△△△△△△

So, Have You Accepted The Truth?

If I could talk to my 14-year-old self who was at that seminar in that camp site, I would say,

"When it comes to masturbation and porn I want you to know that God loves you. God forgives you no matter what. However, He wants you to know that masturbation and porn aren't part of good sex. He has something better. It may sound counter-cultural, it may sound difficult, but He doesn't want us to become dependent on masturbation or porn and slip into a cycle of guilt. I'm telling you this to stop all of the confusion."

Those words would have helped me so much. It took me a long time and a dark destructive cycle until I realised how much masturbation and porn were hurting me. I now realise that acceptance is the first step to freedom. It's vital to acceptance that lusting after women, fantasising about women and masturbating, are wrong. Doing it doesn't make us bad people. God can forgive, but God has a better life for us.

Fundamentally, if we don't accept that we need to change, then we will never change. Don't try to change your patterns of behaviour if you don't really want to; that just doesn't work. But, realise that God wants us to live and act with an understanding of good sex, knowing what will fulfil us and what won't. We want to take away the confusion, the dependency on porn and masturbation, and replace it with things that will build us up rather than break us.

STOP AND REFLECT

- If 100 equals 'I totally agree', and 0 equals 'I totally disagree', what score would you give each of these statements:

  - Watching porn is wrong

  - Masturbation is wrong

  - Looking at women is wrong

  - Looking at women with lustful desires is wrong

- What do you think about the idea that even though you have done wrong, God still loves you?

EXERCISE

After David had slept with Bathsheba he wrote Psalm 51 as a way of saying sorry to God. If you have overstepped the mark, maybe you could read Psalm 51 to God as your way of saying sorry.

Stop and Reflect With Others

- What have you heard other Christian people say about porn and masturbation? Is it okay, or not?

- Did you agree with what this chapter said about porn and masturbation? Talk about how you scored the above statements.

Guilty

You may be reading this book because you feel bad about something you've done or you're still struggling with. Maybe the last chapter was challenging for you and you feel anxious, guilty, and slightly overwhelmed. Well I know what it is like to feel guilty.

The most shameful moment of my life came when I was 18 and travelling around Europe with a friend on a holiday. We'd been travelling for three weeks and ended up in Prague. We booked ourselves into a cheap hostel and spent the next two days wandering round the city, drinking cheap beer and trying not to get lost.

After one particular day of walking around Prague rather aimlessly, we came back to the hostel and were loudly interrupted by two men running out of the women's showers. They were laughing and when we asked what had happened they told us they were trying to see women taking a shower, which shocked us a bit (that isn't normal in any country). One of the men was French, and he invited us into his room. Since we didn't have any plans we accepted. A very large amount of beer was consumed and the conversation got onto our favourite sex positions. I explained that I was a Christian and hadn't had sex yet, which they seemed to be very surprised about.

Eventually the French guy decided that we would go to some bars, and since we had no money everything was on him (he was some big shot city guy supposedly). We got into a taxi and rocked up at the first bar, which turned out to be a strip club – it didn't take much persuasion for me to go in. We had a beer, but the French guy seemed agitated. It turned out that he and his buddy weren't just looking for a strip bar, they were looking for a brothel. So, into another taxi we got and we arrived at a brothel.

I explained to the French guy that I wasn't going to have sex with a prostitute and he said that was fine, we would just go for another beer. I had never been into a brothel before, but there I sat down with our new friends and had another drink.

After thirty minutes in the brothel I gave in. I didn't have penetrative sex, but I went way too far.

The feeling of guilt that greeted me straight after was all consuming. I knew I had screwed up. That guilt didn't leave me for six months. Every time I thought about what I had done I was filled with shame. Every time I tried to pray I just thought about how much I had failed to be a follower of Jesus. Even now I still look back on that moment with deep regret. If I could take back any moment in my entire life it would be that one.

All I could think was that my failures defined me, and my mistakes were my identity. My screw up ruled over me.

The most difficult human emotion I have ever experienced is guilt. Other emotions, such as sadness, can be extremely painful, but no other emotion has come close to the feeling of guilt. The feeling of complete failure and worthlessness. The feeling that continually stays with you day and night for days, weeks and months. The constant whisper inside your head reminding you that you have done something wrong and missed the mark can be, at some points, emotionally and spiritually debilitating. It may look on the outside like everything is fine, but on the inside it feels as if you are being punched when you've already surrendered.

We've probably all been there. Especially if we're thinking about our sexual desires, fantasies, masturbation, porn, and things we did with other people. We may also get feelings of failure, insecurity, loneliness, sadness, anxiety, a lack of self-esteem, embarrassment, remorse, shame, and being trapped in your past. Some people will say guilt is simply something that's constructed by religious people to make you feel bad about having fun. But guilt is more than just a 'killjoy'.

The feeling of guilt is one of the greatest struggles for people trapped in a world of sexual temptation, masturbation, sleeping around and pornography. All we want is for the guilt to go away, but whatever we do, it seems to stay clinging onto us. This guilt can end up destroying us from the inside out, hanging over us for months or years. We just want to know how to be free.

What Can We Do With All This Guilt?

Some people in church say that guilt isn't always a bad thing. Guilt is one of the emotions that can help us to change our lives, and be such a powerful emotion that it brings us back to Jesus. They say that without the feelings of guilt we would find it much harder to realise that what we're doing is wrong and we need someone to help us. Without guilt we would struggle to have the passion and motivation to change our lives radically. Guilt can therefore be a slap in the face that changes our lives for the better and (re)focuses them back on Jesus.

In my experience guilt rarely works in that way.

From my experience, guilt and the shame that often goes with it is like a prison cell. Yes, it does lead me to apologise to Jesus (many times), but guilt rarely leads to a change in my life. Most of the time guilt leads me to my own jail, where I freely lock myself in and throw away the key until eventually enough time passes by and I forgot why I ever locked myself in the cell. Everything in my life is looked at through these bars of guilt. I see myself through these bars of guilt. "I am a failure. I am not good enough". I see my relationship with God through these bars of guilt. "I cannot have a relation-ship with God. God doesn't want me." I see my future through these bars of guilt. "I will never be good enough. I will never achieve anything. I will never become the person God created me to be."

When we mess up and have these feelings of guilt and shame, the feelings can often end up defining our relationship with God and our view of ourselves. We see our relationship with God as good when we have a good week, but our relationship with God as bad when we have a bad week. We feel positive about ourselves and our future when we have a good week, but feel negative and hopeless when we mess up. Sexual sin ends up becoming the barometer of our lives. It defines our moods, our attitude, our spiritual life and our relationships. We place blinkers on our head and all we see is ourselves being defined by whether we looked at porn yesterday or not. We are ruled by our sexual behaviour.

But your screw up doesn't need to define you. Your screw up isn't your identity. Your screw up doesn't rule over you.

God Is With The Guilty

The problem is that we feel bad, and we feel we need to fix it all on our own. We think that if we make everything better with our own will power and our own ideas, then God might love us again.

But the message of Jesus doesn't teach us that, it's the complete opposite! We don't need to be the 'perfect Christian' for God to want to be with us. We are always loved by God and He wants to be with us in the struggle as we begin to be changed by Him. Guilt doesn't lead to condemnation. We're not alone.

There is a famous story Jesus tells of a son who asks his father for his inheritance before he has even died (a bit rude). The son then leaves home and wastes all the money on parties, women, and drink. Soon after, he knows he has messed up, he feels ashamed and guilty, but because he has run out of money and is starving to death he has no choice but to return to his father. The son says, "I will set out and go back to my father and say to him: 'Father, I have sinned against heaven and against you. I am no longer worthy to be called your son; make me like one of your hired servants.'"[10]

I can relate to the son's feelings, because that is how I felt: not worthy to be called a follower of Jesus, not worthy of God's love, not worthy to even be near Him. But the father's response to his son is extraordinary. "So he got up and went to his father. But while he was still a long way off, his father

---

10   Luke 15:18-19

saw him and was filled with compassion for him; he ran to his son, threw his arms around him and kissed him. The son said to him, 'Father, I have sinned against heaven and against you. I am no longer worthy to be called your son.' But the father said to his servants, 'Quick! Bring the best robe and put it on him. Put a ring on his finger and sandals on his feet. Bring the fattened calf and kill it. Let's have a feast and celebrate.'"[11]

The son had messed up but the father was just happy he had come home. The son didn't feel he was good enough but the father still welcomed him back with open arms.

The story of the prodigal son is my story. I mess up, I feel guilty, I don't feel good enough, I don't think God could ever want me – but God runs to me, accepts me, forgives me, doesn't condemn me, and tells me He's just glad I'm home.

The truth is, on our own, we can't do anything with all of this guilt apart from feel bad and alone. But God sees us with love, helps us overcome the guilt, gives us the power to change, provides us the grace when we fail and hands us the strength to fight. He also reminds us that we are more than our sexual desires.

---

11 Luke 15:20-23

A New Perspective

Part of the reason these guilty emotions consume men to such a degree is down to our Christian culture. Christians have unintentionally attached a special status to sexual sin. In a sense, through what they say or don't say, they elevate sexual sin to a height way beyond where it should be. Churches or Christians don't talk about it and sexual sin then becomes like the name 'Voldemort' in Harry Potter. It's so bad that you cannot even mention its name. Men think it must be extremely evil, the majority of us guys have and continue to, or will, struggle with sex, relationships and boundaries, yet Christians and churches stay silent about it. Men often place porn, masturbation, and sex above all other sins precisely because no one is talking about it.

The other side of the coin is the growing awareness of sexual sin by some Christians, churches, and organisations. In one sense this is an amazing development. However, sometimes they can unintentionally become, or appear to be, so completely focused on stopping guys (and girls) looking at porn, that it makes, or appears to make, porn the focus instead of

Jesus. Guys struggle with sexual sin and so look at these organisations' websites, go to their events, read their books and this elevates victory over sexual sin as the pinnacle of Christian life: 'If you can conquer sexual sin, you're a good person.'

I want to say something that may come across as controversial: I don't think that's true.

God cares about some things far more than what you do with your penis. However, lots of men, including me, can act and feel like God cares about nothing else.

That isn't to say sexual sin isn't important: it's very important. I'm writing a book about it because it's important. However, one of the most important truths to discover when struggling with sexual sin is that it doesn't define who you are or your relationship with God.

Feelings of guilt are sometimes not in proportion to the wrong we have done. We often feel more guilt for one thing over another. Guilt is influenced by personal experience, upbringing, character, culture and the church. Most Christian men would place the guilt they feel about sexual sin pretty high, while placing the guilt they feel about not giving money to the poor pretty low. It may surprise you that God actually speaks a lot more about giving to the poor than He does about sex. Yet we feel far more guilty about looking at porn than we do about not giving money to the poor.

We define our lives through how well we are controlling our sexual urges, but I have never heard anyone define their life by how much they give to the poor.

You are not defined by what you do with your penis. God does not place you in a special 'sexual pervert box' that is reserved for people with problems controlling their impulses. So why do you place yourself there?

It's important that guilt and shame doesn't strip us of hope, but it's even more important to recognise who gave us hope in the first place. It's at the very moment when we are faced with a wall of guilt and shame that we recognise we're messed-up and broken people. It's at this moment that we realise we cannot do it alone. We are compelled to run to God and ask for help. It's at this moment we realise we've been found guilty and need to be rescued.

I'm going to talk about the practical things that helped me stop masturbating, looking at porn and treating women like objects instead of human beings. I'm going to be real about how hard it was, and about how I messed up along the way. But I want you to know, guilt and shame will only put you in a prison or make you run from God. But I want you to run towards God!

I want you to know that you're not doing all of this hard work to impress God, you're doing it because God is already impressed by you. He loves you, He accepts you, He sees the potential, and He will help you in the practical, hard, and boring bits.

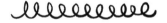

STOP AND REFLECT

- When you look at your own life what makes you feel guilty and ashamed?

  'God showed how much He loved us by sending His one and only Son into the world so that we might have eternal life through Him. This is real love—not that we loved God, but that He loved us and sent His Son as a sacrifice to take away our sins.' (1 John 4:9–10, NLT)

- Do you find it hard to accept that God could love you?

- When you start to feel guilty, what can you do to make sure you run back to God and ask Him for help? For example put Bible verses on your screen saver, have a friend you can text to ask for prayer, memorise a verse of bible, listen to a certain song, something else?

Stop and Reflect With Others

- Do you feel guilt and shame? When and why do you feel these emotions?

- Is there anything in your life you've hidden from everyone that you feel ashamed about?

You're Forgiven, So Act Like It

You are loved. You are forgiven.

You are loved. You are forgiven.

You are loved. You are forgiven.

How do I know that? Imagine, 2000 years ago, we're on the Mount of Olives as it glares in the morning light. The sun has just revealed itself from behind the horizon and Jesus is sat cross-legged at the temple. In front of him are many people, some old and some young, but all are looking intently at Jesus' mouth waiting for his lips to move into motion. Finally, he opens his mouth and begins to speak. People shuffle closer, making sure they don't miss anything that Jesus says.

Suddenly there's a loud noise at the back of the temple and a group of men burst in dragging a young woman with them.

She looks as if she has barely got dressed, her hair's tangled and she looks scared. She whimpers softly as the men throw her into the huddle of people listening to Jesus. They quickly part as she falls to the ground in front of him. One of the men shouts in a mocking tone, "Teacher, this woman was caught in the act of adultery. The Law of Moses says to stone her. What do you say?"

Jesus looks carefully at the woman. The young woman is still lying on the floor, hiding her face. Briefly she looks up at Jesus and he sees the complete fear in her eyes, but she quickly looks away again. The men are still shouting, "Teacher, what should we do?" Jesus ignores their shouts and continues to look upon this hopeless young woman laying in front of him. After a while, as the shouts are getting louder, Jesus begins to speak.

"You can stone this woman, but let the person that has never sinned throw the first stone". Immediately the men stop shouting. The whole temple descends into silence.

Slowly, one of the older men slips out of the temple. He's followed quickly by another man, and before long all the accusers have left. All that remains is the young woman. Jesus takes the young woman's hand and helps her to her feet. He looks upon her desperate state and softly says, "Where are the men that accuse you? Did even one man find you guilty?" She slowly looks around, but can't see any of them. "No, Lord", she mutters.

Jesus stares directly at her and speaks compassionately, "Then I do not find you guilty. Go and live a life free from sin".[12]

The bible doesn't say what happens to the woman after Jesus rescues her. Maybe her life was transformed. Maybe she never committed adultery again. Maybe she went back to her old life. No one knows. But what we do know is that Jesus rescued the woman from death. He saved her, he freed her. I suspect his actions on that day changed her forever. A guilty woman comes to Jesus and a free woman leaves.

---

12   Story based on John 8:1-11

Jesus Forgives Her

The story tells of an adulterous woman getting thrown before Jesus. (For some reason, the man wasn't dragged out and humiliated!) I suspect the woman wished she had been able to meet Jesus under better circumstances. She probably wished she could have got dressed, brushed her hair, put on some perfume and made herself look presentable. But the woman is brought before Jesus under the backdrop of her most shameful moment. She is brought before Jesus as the worst moment of her life is made public. She is brought before Jesus broken, disgraced, and guilty. She's lost all dignity and worth.

I guess many of us wish we could meet Jesus, without all our baggage hanging around our neck. I suspect many of us wish we could meet with Jesus without having to bring along what happened last night, last week, or last month. We all want to meet Jesus as the perfect version of ourselves, the one that didn't mess up, the one that didn't look at porn.

But Jesus, because he sees it all, knows us and what we've done. In many ways our stories are similar to this adulterous woman's. We've messed up. We've looked at porn, we've masturbated, we've had sex outside marriage, and we've lusted after women. We've missed the mark.

We don't come to Jesus as people that have it sorted or people that are perfect. We come to Jesus as people that are broken.

Yet Jesus accepts, forgives, and helps us, like he did with the woman in the story.

~~~~~~~~~

Jesus Forgives You

I know that as I stand before Jesus I'm guilty. Guilty of adultery. Guilty of looking at porn. Guilty of lusting after women. I know it and Jesus knows it. I guess you can probably relate to this too.

We can't just hide our problems or wish them away, Jesus sees the real you. He sees your thoughts and feelings; he sees your actions when you are alone. He sees everything, but Jesus accepts, forgives and helps you.

Jesus was the only guy that ever lived a perfect life. He was the only person who will ever live and do nothing wrong – he was not guilty of anything. He never lusted after anyone. He then chooses to die a horrifically painful death on a cross. As he was pinned to the cross in agonising pain, he lets out his final breath and he exchanges his life for our lives. He trades his perfect life for our imperfect lives.

It was at that precarious moment hanging between life and death that Jesus took ownership for my sin, past, present and future. At that moment, he took responsibility for the boy that first masturbated at 12. He accepted the punishment for the man that visited the prostitute. He suffered the guilt of the teenager who kept looking at porn and masturbating. He took everything that I have ever and will ever do wrong. He took responsibility for it all, and as he passed from life into death my failures were taken with him.

If you follow Jesus, he did exactly the same for you. He took responsibility for everything wrong you have done or will do. He took the blame for the times you looked at porn. He took the punishment for the times you had sex with your girlfriend. He took the penalty for the darkest moments of your life. He took the punishment for things we haven't even done yet.

Jesus was found guilty in your place and took the punishment. He traded his perfect life, for your imperfect life. He traded his purity for your adultery.

As we stand before God the Father we're guilty. We're guilty of adultery. But it's in this moment that the Father utters the most incredible words, "I do not find you guilty, Jesus took the guilt for your screw ups. Now go and live a life free from sin."

This is the beginning and the end in a man's fight against being controlled by his penis. Jesus saves you, Jesus rescues you and Jesus frees you.

- - - - - - - - - - - - - -

You Need To Forgive You

I said earlier that sexual sin and the guilt associated with it can feel as though you're trapped in a prison cell. It feels as if whatever you do you can't break the endless cycle of doing the wrong thing.

You're stuck in a prison cell of guilt, disappointment, failure and worthlessness. Sometimes you may forget that you're in the cell and feel more positive about life, but it doesn't take long for you to mess up and realise that you're not free.

What Jesus did 2000 years ago was to break open the prison cell doors, he set you free, but many of us are still in the cell.

For some people the hardest thing to understand about Christianity is that you can be forgiven. Everything wrong that you have ever done or will do in your life can be wiped off your record. For others, the hardest thing about Christianity isn't understanding that Jesus has forgiven me, but that I need to forgive me.

You know Jesus has fought for you, forgiven you, but you haven't forgiven yourself yet. Your past is constantly in your present and you still see yourself as a failure.

There's an illustration I heard once of a young man who was sent to prison. He had lived a life of crime, but everyday felt sorry for what he had done and how they had affected the people involved. He even scrawled his crimes into the concrete walls as a constant reminder of what he had done. One day, after writing a letter and explaining to the judge that he felt sorry and wished it could all be different, the judge surprisingly came to him and told him he was free to leave.

He opened the cell door and said, "whenever you want, you're free to go, I will leave the cell door open". A few minutes went by and the young man just stared at the open door. Hours, days, and weeks went by and the young man had not moved from his cell.

After a few months the judge came back and asked the young man why he hadn't walked free. The young man replied, "when I think about everything I have done, I don't deserve to be free. I deserve to die in my cell".

The judge looked at him for a few moments and began to speak, "I spent millions of pounds to fight for your freedom. I risked my career, my family, my house, my happiness on you. I managed to get your criminal records wiped clean. I have even officially adopted you as my son and set up a bedroom in my house for you to live when you get out". The judge paused "When you first wrote to me you wished for your freedom and a new start. I gambled everything to give you that new life. Did you even really want it?"

To escape our prison cells we need to understand that God, the judge, our defender, our new father, our friend, has forgiven us. The only thing stopping us now is if we refuse to forgive ourselves. For much of my life I was keeping myself in the prison, even though the door was open.

MMMMMMMM

Our Identity Isn't In The Battle

When we're struggling with sexual sin, it's very hard for us to see anything other than this seemingly massive problem in our life. Often, it's accompanied by a constant feeling of guilt, shame, and failure, and it becomes hard to look outside of ourselves. We either constantly want to give in or we're constantly feeling guilty about the last time we gave in. The fight that rages inside of us becomes so ferocious that it overtakes everything else in our life.

Instead of sexual actions, thoughts, and feelings being a part of our life, they become our whole life, our focus, our goal, our hope.

This could be because sex takes up so much head space that we live our whole lives around trying to gratify our sexual desires and getting our next fix. Or it could be that we focus all of our attention on trying to win the fight against our sexual urges, that we lose focus on everything and everyone else. Or in my case, it would be a mixture of the two.

In this fierce battle we can often lose complete perspective on who and what is important in life, and instead become consumed in the fight. Yes, I tried to follow Jesus, but from my perspective I didn't do a very good job. I kept getting it wrong. So how could God accept me? But what I have had to learn the hard way is that God accepts, wants, and loves me despite my self-control problems.

Illogical Acceptance

I now have a little daughter. Being a parent is far harder work than it is in the movies, but when you have a kid, you get this strange bond between you. I love my daughter and I can say with complete certainty that I will always love my daughter. She could turn into the worst teenager imaginable and I would still love her. She could become a drug-dealing murderer and I would still love her. It doesn't make any logical sense, but whatever she does I will always accept, want, and love her for no other reason than this; she is my daughter.

God is our father. It makes absolutely no logical sense why He would accept, want, and love us. But the truth is that He loves us no matter what. We could look at porn 24 hours a day and He would still love us. Not because we deserve it, but simply because He's our dad.

Obviously, He wants us to change. He wants us to be the best we can be. He wants us to turn from our problems and live a life that is truly amazing. He wants us to stop looking at porn and masturbating. But when we do mess up, He still loves us because He's our dad.

We are God's children and whether we accept it yet or not. We will always be accepted, wanted, and loved by God.

— · — , — · —

Your Identity Is In A Loving God

Many of us live as if God could never accept someone like 'me'. That was certainly true in my case. I couldn't see past my failures as a person and thought that God must see me the way I see myself. I couldn't stop looking at porn and masturbating, so I thought, how could God want me?

I couldn't follow Jesus very well so thought God could never love someone like me. And I tried and I tried and I tried to stop looking at porn, to stop masturbating, and to stop all the mess in my life because I thought that when I did God would finally accept me and I could then be a "good" Christian.

The problem was that however hard I tried I couldn't stop all the mess in my life, but the bigger problem was that I could never understand how God could want someone like me.

And for many years I sat in that hopeless, dark place trying and failing to be good enough for God.

I thought that was how others saw me, my identity, and my label, was in my failure.

But freedom in life doesn't come when you have everything sorted. Freedom in life comes when you realise that God wants you even if nothing in your life is sorted. I still don't have everything perfect, I always thought that the older you get the fewer problems you have, and you naturally start to sin less.

That's rubbish though. Age doesn't bring an automatic sin shield or a way to make everything perfect. I still mess up, I still get things wrong, but I know that God accepts, wants and loves me.

My identity isn't in my actions, my successes, my feelings or my failures. My identity is in a God of Love, who has forgiven me and accepts me because He wants me, loves me and will never give up on me.

This understanding isn't just in my head, but deep down into the core of me. It has changed my life, and it can change yours.

Your identity is not in your battle, but in God and in His forgiveness and acceptance.

○○●○○●○○●○○●

STOP AND REFLECT

- Describe your relationship with God in five words.

- What words would God use to describe you? Forgiven, chosen, holy, loved, accepted, useful, child, heir, freed, wanted, pure?

- Which word do you find the hardest to accept?

'And I am convinced that nothing can ever separate us from God's love. Neither death nor life, neither angels nor demons, neither our fears for today nor our worries about tomorrow—not even the powers of hell can separate us from God's love. No power in the sky above or in the earth below —indeed, nothing in all creation will ever be able to separate us from the love of God that is revealed in Christ Jesus our Lord.' (Romans 8:38–39 NLT)

Exercise

Write down everything you feel ashamed about - then cross everything off the list. Remind yourself how God really sees you.

Stop and Reflect With Others

- Why do people find it hard to accept that God could love them?

- Which words did you use to describe your relationship with God?

- Which word that God uses about you, do you find the hardest to accept?

Living God's Way

It was a warm day for the middle of winter and the sun was shining over my keyboard. I was just having a look on social media when all of a sudden a picture catches my eye. A flash of skin and my body (or specifically my penis) begins to wake up.

I go to the search bar and pause for a second. I know I shouldn't. I know this is wrong. I'm not going to look at porn today. Over the next few seconds my mind starts whispering to me, "Ben just have a quick look. Ten seconds and then you will have satisfied your urge and can get back to watching cat videos".

But this time I'm determined not to do it. I'm determined to stay strong; I'm going to hold out against it.

Over the next few seconds the feeling gets stronger and the whispers become louder. It's as if every part of my body is screaming out to give in. I take a deep breath, try to think of dead badgers and in desperation I pray. But the feeling inside me gets stronger and stronger until I can't bear it anymore. I click on the search bar, type in a familiar few words, click enter and it's done.

Then the whisper says 'you failed again'.

God's View Of Sex

Finding freedom from being controlled by your sexual desires and impulses is easier said than done. For many of us it's a constant fight. We try not to mess up, but however hard we try, it doesn't seem to help. This isn't made any easier by the fact that pictures and videos of naked woman are so accessible.

Since the invention of the internet you can easily find pictures, even if you're not trying. It's, for the most part, completely free and there is virtually no chance of someone catching you.

(Saying that, my mum did once catch me looking at pictures, which was slightly awkward and pretty much impossible to explain. I was on the computer, which was upstairs and didn't hear her coming up the stairs 'til the last moment. The reaction on her face was complete shock and I was probably more embarrassed than any other time in my life. In that moment I did what all "real men" do – I quickly went to my room to hide from my mum. I ignored it and hoped she would forget about it.)

Porn is now more accessible than it's ever been. While looking at porn and masturbating is unhelpful, there's a deeper underlying thing happening every time we watch porn or masturbate. It's the underlying effect that makes it wrong and unhelpful. Porn and masturbation create a fantasy world where we're the centre. It makes sex about 'me' and not 'us'. The women we look at stop becoming people, and we make it all about what 'I' want.

When we look at porn the world stops revolving around God and His design for sex, and it starts revolving around 'me'. In this fantasy world we look at what we want, whenever we want, as often as we want. Sex becomes about 'me and my needs'. We think the women we look at belong to us. We think nothing is off limits.

But God designed sex to be between two hearts, two minds, and two bodies, where people are committed to each other in marriage, put each others needs first and respect each other.[13]

~~~~~~~~~

Your Heart

In the passage from Matthew, Jesus says:

"But I say to you that everyone who looks at a woman with lustful intent has already committed adultery with her in his heart."[14]

In the Bible the word 'heart' is used to describe a person's thoughts, feelings, desires, personality, conscience, and spiritual life. It represents everything that makes you, you. It's who you are and affects everything you do and say, both good and bad. It's because of your 'heart' that you do right

---

13   1 Corinthians 7:1-5, Ephesians 5:21-33
14   Matthew 5:28 NLT

and wrong things. The root of all human behaviour is their 'heart'.[15]

When we look at porn or masturbate the underlying problem is our 'heart'. Our thoughts, feelings, desires, personality, conscience, and spiritual life, turn away from God and His design instead of towards Him.

Many people struggle to stop because they think that they can change their behaviour without changing their thoughts, desires, and feelings. To change our behaviour, we must first change where that behaviour comes from.

For example, no one would try to stop a boat with a hole from sinking by simply using a bucket to bail water out. It may work short term, but in the long term, it's only going to end with everybody sinking. Fixing the hole is the only way to stop the boat from sinking. It's the same with our behaviour. Long term we must change our heart to change our behaviour.

The good news is that when we become a follower of Jesus he gives us a new heart – we get a new life.[16] We get this

---

15   See Genesis 6:5, Proverbs 4:23, Jeremiah 17:9, 24:7, James 3:14
16   See Deuteronomy 30:6, Ezekiel 11:19, 36:26, Romans 6:4, 17

new heart and new life as a free gift from God, not because of how good or bad we are, but simply because we become part of God's family. This doesn't mean everything is amazing and we never have to struggle with anything ever again, but it means God brings us into his family and stays with us during the good and messy bits of our lives. But it doesn't mean we don't struggle.

As I have found out, this new life actually means that we have another struggle and this is the biggest fight of them all. We have a fight between our God given new life that wants to follow Jesus and worship him as God, and our old life that wants to stick a finger up at God, do its own thing and make the world about 'me'.

This constant struggle will be with us until we die and Jesus perfects us, but until then we are forced to fight with our old self that wants to rebel.

Fight Club

I went to Thailand a few years ago with my wife to learn Muay Thai boxing. It's a brutal sport and the training is even more brutal. We trained for six hours every day in 30°C+ heat and 90%+ humidity. Every day I would come back to the hotel battered and bruised. Day after day I would punch, kick, elbow and knee bags over and over again, until my body broke down and I wanted to cry. The fights are insane, mainly involving lots of blood and the constant sound of bodies hitting the canvas.

When I arrived in Thailand I had no idea what I was doing. I had never punched anybody before (other than family) and I'm about as violent as a butterfly watching 'The Bake Off'. The trainers took my wife and I off to a separate part of the gym and for days taught us how to punch, block, and kick. After a few days we were allowed into the beginner class and after a few more days we started sparring.

To start with we weren't very good at boxing. When we began sparring we got hit a lot, but the trainers didn't start yelling at us and making us do 100 press-ups. We had only just begun to learn how to fight. Over the month we were there we got slightly better and every so often we managed to hit someone else rather than our faces being used as a punch bag. We began to get fitter, stronger, more intelligent, able to defend ourselves and every so often not get beaten. At first boxing seemed impossible. We had no idea how to fight, but the more we did it the easier it became.

For many of us the fight against our desires seems impossible. We feel like I did when I started boxing: weak, feeble, and unable to do anything but lose. I used to pray all the time for God to free me from my desires, but in my experience God didn't step in and win every fight for me, even though He was always with me. Trying to stop looking at porn, masturbating and having inappropriate sex is hard work. God is not naïve, He realises it's difficult, but His desire for us is to keep going, to keep picking ourselves back up and to keep fighting with Him and for Him.

When we fight the urge to watch porn, to masturbate, to give in to lust, we make a choice to fight for the 'Jesus way'. Like I said, God gives us a new heart, He rescues us and He changes us. He's the focus. But we need to choose to follow Him and live His way. We have to choose to let Him into our lives, our hearts and our mess.

We're involved in the process.

We're not a passive spectator somewhere in the crowd. We're involved in the fight. The good news is that when we continue to fight for Jesus and with Jesus, the fight will become easier. We will begin to start winning, we will begin to find freedom and we will begin to discover our new heart.

In the next chapter I want to outline some practical tips and advice which helped me to fight and choose Jesus when it came to sex and relationships. I want you to be ready for the fight, and I want you to live the life you were created to live, which is better than we could ever hope for.

When we mess up, there is forgiveness, and God is always with us. His love for us isn't rooted in our success. But we need to decide to follow Him, and to fight.

Stop and Reflect

- What parts of your old life are at war with your new life? This could include more than just porn and masturbation.

- 'Above all else, guard your heart, for everything you do flows from it.' (Proverbs 4:23)

- What does it mean for you to guard your heart? Is anything in your life trying to attack or hurt your heart?

- In what ways can you make your world revolve around God every day? For example, before falling asleep every night thank God for three things that happened in that day.

Stop and Reflect With Others

- Share one part of your old life that is at war with your new life.

- If you were in a boxing ring with your sexual desires, is it a close fight or are you generally winning or losing? Why?

Let's Get Practical

I remember the feeling of failure. I remember being determined that I would never look at porn again and I remember getting angry at God and asking Him, "Why don't you take away all these wrong desires?" After a day or so my determination would go, God didn't take away my feelings of lust, and I would slip up again.

If I learnt anything in my years of struggle it's that pure will-power never helped much and God never just clicked His fingers and made all these lustful thoughts and feelings disappear. I needed some practical tips; I needed to take some practical steps to bring change, and these tools still help me today. God was with me every step of the way, but I had to learn to make different choices. The good news is, anyone can do what I did. There are small things that we can all put into our lives that make a big difference in our fight against porn, masturbation, lust, and everything else that ultimately destroys us.

The first thing that helped me was understanding why I wanted to keep watching porn, and what was going on in my mind.

•-•-•-•••-•-••-•-••-•••-•

Can Anyone Be Dependent On Porn?

In the mid-20th century smoking was common in Britain. By the 1960s 70% of men and 43% of women smoked and most people were unaware of the dangers of smoking.[17] In fact, some doctors used to endorse cigarettes as being good for you. One of the most famous campaigns of this era was the "More Doctors" campaign for Camels cigarettes. These adverts claimed that according to a nationwide survey, "More doctors smoke Camels than any other cigarette!" There was even an advertising campaign run by Winston's encouraging pregnant women to smoke: "Winston when you're smoking for two". Shocking, right?

Nowadays we look back and think, how could people not know that smoking was damaging for your health? Were they tricking people on purpose?

---

17 Evans, M. (2012) Smoking - 50 years of progress but not worldwide, Accessed 11 April 2018. http://www.earthtimes.org/health/smoking-50-years-progress-worldwide/1862/#ipmorRKb8ZHpIBuo.99

The reality is, cigarette companies, doctors, and health experts genuinely didn't always know that smoking was bad for your health. It was only when new medical, technological, and scientific research was completed that they realised there were direct links to cancer and other health risks.

For a long time, people have believed that porn isn't harmful and have said things like, "It's just a bit of fun, what's the big deal?" However, the long-term impact of porn on your mind is beginning to be understood and the findings are showing that pornography is both damaging and can cause dependency, some would even say it's addictive. Many people don't want to believe it. Just like many people didn't want to believe cigarettes were harmful. However, the more scientists learn about the impact of porn, the more we understand that porn isn't just harmless fun. Chemical reactions are happening in our bodies and in our brains.

When we watch porn we release a chemical into our body called dopamine. Now, dopamine is produced by our bodies naturally and it helps control the brain's pleasure and reward centres. It makes us want to do things that sustain our lives and makes us feel good after we have done them.

So if I go for a run, the reward centre in my brain sends out signals and chemicals (dopamine) to my body which make me feel good afterwards. The high that we feel after going for a run, eating food, or having sex is all down to dopamine and dopamine drives us to do the activity again.

The problem is that our reward centre can be hijacked to release dopamine when we take drugs, smoke cigarettes and watch porn, which can then create a dependency or addiction. Dopamine is the drug that makes us want to watch porn and forces us to chase it. Every time we watch porn and click on a new image or video, our dopamine level shoots up.

With the invention of the internet, there is an unlimited amount of new images for people to see. Unlimited novelty means unlimited new waves of dopamine that drive us to watch more, click more, crave more and very quickly, we find ourselves trapped. 'Internet pornography has been called the crack-cocaine of sex addiction, and people in the field of internet addiction say that pornography is the most addictive substance available online'.[18]

18   Hall, P. (2016) Confronting Porn. Durham: McKnight & Bishop. P68.

So, what are the negative side-effects of porn? Is all this dopamine running through our bodies bad?

Well one of the most damaging side effects is that porn re-wires our brain. God created our brain to release dopamine as a reward for doing things that sustain life, like exercise, eating, etc. However, when we watch porn the brain becomes rewired to think that porn is one of those essential, life-sustaining and comforting activities, meaning our body rewards us with a dose of dopamine. This creates a pathway in our brain that eventually make this behaviours and thought pattern automatic.

The high levels of dopamine we get while watching porn make our brains think that porn is really, really, really important, and we should do it again and again. We become dependent and struggle to stop watching it. And like anyone hooked on drugs, we need a bigger fix to get the same high. We begin to need more of it and darker versions of it to reach the same highs. We begin to become desensitized to porn and so our behaviour and preferences escalate in order to chase the same experience and high.

The result of this rewiring in our brains means that we may have difficulties becoming sexually aroused without porn. There may even be increased amounts of depression, tiredness, and anxiety, and we may struggle to be around women without sexually objectifying them.

Porn scientifically changes our brain, it changes the way we think and ultimately it robs us of life.

But don't panic! The wonderful thing about how God created our brain is that even if our brain has been rewired by porn, even if we have become dependent on porn, our brain can rewire itself again. Our brain can sort itself out and we can live lives that aren't controlled by porn, dopamine, and the constant clicking for new material.

STOP AND REFLECT

- Have you ever felt that dopamine high?

- Have a think about the times after you've watched porn. Did you feel as though you needed to watch it? Did you feel like you had any control over your mind?

- Do you think porn can be addictive?

- In your experience has porn been addictive?

- Go to fightthenewdrug.org and yourbrainonporn.com and watch some of the videos about the science of porn

//////////////////

Why Has My Porn Habit Got Worse?

Most people don't begin their journey into the world of porn by watching hard-core porn for six hours every day and masturbating 'til they drop. I certainly didn't. You begin by gradually looking at things that are slightly riskier and you slowly begin to masturbate more often.

You may start by getting your fix from social media images or YouTube videos, but over time that doesn't satisfy you anymore. So you move onto pictures of naked women, then to porn websites and before you know it, you're looking at stuff that once upon a time you would have been disgusted at.

Scientists call this 'escalation'. What excited you before is no longer enough; you want more, you need more. In other words, over time, the little things build into a big thing, and you may not even realise it's happening.

For example, I play tennis and have done so since I was five. The serve in tennis is very important and generally, the faster the serve the better. When I was nine or ten I couldn't serve very fast. I remember when I was about 15 this all changed. After a match my opponent said, "Have you been having loads of lessons? Because you've got a big serve." I hadn't really noticed that my serve had got particularly faster. But over time it had got a little faster, then a little faster again, then a little faster still, and in that moment it dawned on me that I had a big serve. Now, I didn't wake up one day able to serve at 120mph, but over time the little changes built into a big change, I just hadn't noticed.

It's the same with porn – we often don't realise how serious our problem is until we lose the fight. We don't realise that every fight we lose is another little step down the path to our big metaphorical prison cell. We often don't realise that we're even on the path to prison until the door is swung shut behind us. People don't wake up one day in a world consumed by their need for sexual gratification – we take small steps, we lose little fights, and we often don't get serious until it's too late.

The quicker you get serious about defeating this, the easier it is. It may be that you don't feel like what you're doing is too bad, but if you're thinking, looking, fantasising, watching, or touching a woman that isn't your wife, then you are on the path to that prison. You need to get serious before you end up trapped in there.

After I masturbated and watched porn for the first time, I took lots more small steps. For six years I lost seemingly insignificant battles, until I ended up living a life saturated with fake, joyless, screen sex. The little things built into a big thing. It's at that moment where I felt trapped and I realised that I needed to change that I got serious. It's when we hit rock bottom that we know we need to change, but, frustratingly, it's at rock bottom that it can be the hardest to change.

If only we'd got serious before we found ourselves there, trapped and seemingly alone. The time to get serious is now, the time to follow Jesus is now and the time to fight is now. Life is all about little steps – little steps towards Jesus or little steps away from him – where will you step?

STOP AND REFLECT

- Draw a timeline of how your behaviour has changed from when you first looked at porn to now – think about how often you watch, how you watch, has the role of masturbation changed, has any behaviour become riskier, has your sexual behaviour or attitude towards or with others changed. Have these things increased over time?

- Do you need to get serious now?

- What little step can you take this week to de-escalate your behaviour? Or another way of putting it, what little battle can you win this week?

Stop and Reflect With Others

- How did you first start watching porn?

- How has your behaviour changed since then? Talk through your timeline

- If your timeline continued one year into the future, what would you like to write?

Where Does God Fit Into All Of This?

I wish I could tell you that you just have to pray and then everything will be easy, but that's not how it worked for me.

I don't think I could have ever escaped from my life of porn, guilt, and masturbation on my own. I honestly believe that without God, I would still be trapped. God was with me, God helped me and God changed me, but God didn't magic everything away. I had to give God two things for change to happen; time and space.

We live in a world where we want everything now. If I have to wait longer than three minutes at McDonald's I will probably have a moan, "This isn't fast food!" I think I always hoped that God would click His fingers and make all my problems go away, but that never happened. I used to get angry with God and tell Him that if He didn't want me watching porn He should just take away my desire to watch porn. To tell you the truth I believe that God did help me, in a different way, but it took time. It wasn't an overnight transformation, it took years of little steps and little victories for me to find freedom.

It was over this time that God changed me. I learned that I had to let Him in and give Him the space to work. I often find life busy and stressful. Due to this busyness, stress, and distraction, it's often easy to ignore God. When we're caught up in the world of porn and masturbation, it's often very difficult to be with God. God wants to change us. God wants to change our hearts and our desires. God wants to lead us out of our mess, but we have to give God space in our lives and our hearts to do that. We need to take practical steps towards God. The God that I have come to know rarely forces Himself on us, He waits until we open ourselves to Him and then He gets to work.

So often in my life things have got in the way or I've been too busy, too tired or too ashamed to let Him in.

One of the most significant steps that happened on my road to freedom was giving God space to work in my heart. For each person that might look different. For some people, that might be sitting in a room with some worship music on, for others it might be watching a sunset, and for others it might be reading a book. It doesn't matter how you do it but the more we give God space, the more He has opportunities to change us. It will take time, but I believe in a God who can transform death into life, darkness into light and addictions into freedom.

'Since you have heard about Jesus and have learned the truth that comes from him, throw off your old sinful nature and your former way of life, which is corrupted by lust and deception. Instead, *let the Spirit renew your thoughts and attitudes.* Put on your new nature, created to be like God— truly righteous and holy.' (Ephesians 4:21–24 NLT, Italics added)

STOP AND REFLECT

- In our battle with porn, what do you expect from God?

- Has God met your expectations or not? If not, why do you think that might be?

- Have you ever asked God why He hasn't met your expectations?

- 'Three times I pleaded with the Lord to take it away from me. But He said to me, "My grace is sufficient for you, for my power is made perfect in weakness…' (2 Corinthians 12:8–9)

- When do you feel closest to God? Up a mountain, listening to music, talking to others, reading your bible, at church, helping others or something else? Challenge yourself and do this as much a possible this week.

Stop and Reflect With Others

- What do you think of the sentence: 'God was with me, God helped me and God changed me, but God didn't magic everything away.' Has that been your experience?

- Do you find it easy or difficult giving God time and space in your life? Why?

Do I Really Need To Tell Anyone Else?

The first time I ever told anyone I struggled with looking at porn and masturbating was when I was 18, years after I had first started. One of the most difficult aspects of fighting sexual sin is that, for the most part, it all happens in private.

A person can spend all night looking at porn and then rock up to church the next day and no one would ever know. A person can spend their whole life trapped in sin and hide it so well that no one would know. It seems easy for people to get alongside us and help us through other struggles in life such as relationships, anger, grief, physical injury, or unemployment. The sad part about sexual sin is that, for the most part, people fight it alone and without support. People up and down the country are living in a world of guilt, shame and entrapment and they haven't told anyone.

One of the most freeing things a human can do is to tell someone their deepest, darkest secret. In the act of telling someone it seems as though it's no longer so deep, so dark, or so secret. It feels as if something that has been constantly eating you up on the inside has been let out. It feels as if you have been freed from your past and can live in the hope of your future.

I have thought for a long time that if you cannot share something about your life (in the right setting) then it still has some hold over you. If you cannot talk about your sexual sin with someone that you trust, then it still has some control over you. Free men can talk about their past mistakes and troubles because they are left in the past. Trapped men cannot talk about their past mistakes and troubles because they are still their present.

'Whoever conceals their sins does not prosper, but the one who confesses and renounces them finds mercy.' (Proverbs 28:13)

It may seem like no one else would understand what you are going through. Will they just laugh at me? Will they judge me? Will they kick me out of church? Questions like these are normal and I don't know anyone who wouldn't be scared and nervous about sharing this, but it's important. You may choose to talk to a church leader, it may be a youth worker, it may be a close friend, it may be a family member or it may even be an old dude in church.

Here are a few practical guidelines for choosing someone to talk to:

1. Preferably a man – for both of you these conversations are normally more appropriate if you are the same sex. (If you only have a female leader, she can point you to someone you may have overlooked.)

2. They should be committed to following Jesus in their own life.

3. It's generally best if you already know the person and can trust them.

No one enjoys telling people their mistakes. No one enjoys telling people intimate parts of their life, but I found that freedom comes from bringing stuff out of the darkness and into the light.

— — — — —

STOP AND REFLECT

- Have you ever told anyone about your struggle? If not, what is holding you back?

- Who could you tell? List everyone that fits the criteria above - family, friends, youth worker, church leader, old dude, etc. Now look at the list and choose one person you could tell.

lllllllll

Why Do I Struggle To Resist The Temptation?!

It feels almost as if something goes off deep inside of you and you no longer have control over your body. You get triggered by something. It could be the flash of skin, stress, a picture on the internet, boredom, a specific time of day, it could be anything but something goes off inside you.

You change from being in control of your sexual desire to your sexual desire being in control of you.

And over the next few seconds, minutes, hours, days, or weeks, this sexual desire grows. It becomes all-consuming until you feel like you have no choice but to give in.

Every person who has tried to fight against sexual temptation will have experienced this sensation. One minute you feel in control of yourself and the next you feel as though there is zero control. The red mist of lust, desire and self-gratification has descended and it feels like there is nothing you can do about it. You've been triggered. Something has gone off inside of you that has triggered a whole host of uncontrollable emotions and desires to rise up within you, which you feel as if you cannot control and will only end in you 'acting out'.

Broadly speaking there are two different types of triggers; internal triggers and external triggers. Internal triggers are those that come from inside us. For example, stress, boredom, loneliness, tiredness or anger, to name a few. External triggers are those that come from outside of us. For example, late night internet surfing, a friend, certain social media apps, glancing at the front page of a magazine.

Everybody has different triggers, but if we manage to identify some of them, we can begin to take practical steps and try to control, and even prevent them. For example, one of my triggers was being up late at night, bored and just surfing the internet with no purpose. There was a good chance that if I did that, or even if I do that now, I would get triggered. The solution to this is to leave my phone downstairs when I go to bed, so the trigger doesn't have a chance to affect me.

We need to know what our triggers are, then we can take practical steps to avoid them.

STOP AND REFLECT

- What are your triggers? Stress, boredom, loneliness, tiredness or anger, late night internet surfing, a friend, social media apps, glancing at the front page of a magazine?

- For each of your triggers, think about how can you best avoid it? Are there any boundaries you can create that might help you? For example, don't go on the internet past a certain time at night. Or don't even take your phone to bed.

Stop and Reflect With Others

- Talk through your own triggers and the boundaries you want to create that might help you stop being triggered as often.

- Set a reminder on your phone to text each other and ask how it's going.

What Should I Do If I Feel Triggered?

However hard you may try to control triggers in your life, it's very likely that you will get triggered. Getting triggered normally meant that I gave in to it shortly afterwards. But it doesn't have to be that way. Just because you get triggered, doesn't mean that you have to mess up and 'act out', there is another option. What's important is that you STOP:

Stop – Stop doing whatever you are doing and take some deep breaths.

Think – Think about what's important to you. Who did God create you to be? What's at risk if you follow through? What's valuable to you?

Other – In order to take your mind off wanting to 'act out', you need to do something else for 20 minutes, that will keep your full attention. Like going for a run, going to the gym, phoning a friend, or listening to music.

Pray – God never clicked His fingers for me, but I believe that God is with us and wants to help us even in the moments we want to walk away from Him. When we get triggered we pray because God will help us.

You might have to go through S.T.O.P ten times per day, for others it might only be once per year. It's always a good idea to chat through with someone else why, when, and what happened after you got triggered, because we're not in this alone.

· ·· ··· ·· ·· ·· ·· ·· ·

Stop and Reflect

- How often are you triggered? Do you have a plan for when you get triggered?

- List some questions you could 'THINK' about that help you gain perspective.

- List what 'OTHER' activities you could do that will fully engage your mind.

Stop and Reflect With Others

- Discuss your lists together.

- When was the last time you were triggered? Why did you get triggered and did it lead to anything?

Does Watching Porn Mean Going Back To Square One?

I can still remember the times that I thought I was on track, where I thought that I had escaped, but then I messed up. My journey to where I am today (and I'm in no way perfect now) was never a straight road. It involved many bumps in the road, times I slipped up and times I allowed old thought patterns and behaviours to creep in. When this happened, my automatic reaction was, "I'm never going to beat this so what is the point in even trying?" It was as if I had fallen back to square one and any and all progress I had made was meaningless. I felt as though I might as well give up.

I dropped back into my prison cell and felt awful about myself and who I was.

I think it's important to understand that your journey to freedom will not be a smooth ride. It's important to recognise that it's a journey. Just because you want to break free, doesn't mean you won't slip up along the way. We will all face bumps and setbacks and for some people, the road will be longer and have more bumps, but I always found two things helpful to remember in the times that I slipped up.

Firstly, just because you've slipped up a little bit doesn't mean you have to go the whole way. It's tempting to think, I've looked at something now, so I might as well find a porn site and masturbate and go the whole way. I mean I've already messed up, so what is the difference in completely messing up?

Having a small slip and then stopping it going any further is a really positive step. Pulling the handbrake up when you're half way down a steep hill is difficult. So when we manage to stop that shows that we have grown. It shows great strength and courage. Having a small slip isn't positive, but managing to stop it going any further is progress. So, when you cross a boundary, when you go too far, when you slip up, it shows strength, courage, and progress when you can stop it going further, and/or get back on track quickly.

We can ask God to help us, we're not on our own, no matter how much we have slipped and gone across the boundary.

Secondly, your journey to freedom will take time but it's also important to remember that the journey back to square one will take time too. I remember when I thought I had come a long way, I hadn't watched porn or masturbated for a couple of weeks and I thought, I've cracked it! Then I would get triggered and end up watching porn and masturbating. I'd feel awful and feel like I'd gone back to square one. I acted like those two weeks without porn didn't matter anymore and I'd have to start again from the bottom.

But you don't go back to square one.

Yes, it's a step backwards, but it's only a small step. If you get back on track and continue your journey forwards you will quickly overcome that small step backwards. The danger is that you think you go back to square one and then binge on old habits and behaviours. You go through a period of days, weeks, and months where you give up and give in.

When you mess up it's only a small step backwards. Pick yourself up and get back on track.

Nelson Mandela said, "Do not judge me by my successes, judge me by how many times I fell down and got back up again."

Stop and Reflect

"The LORD is my shepherd; I have all that I need. He lets me rest in green meadows; he leads me beside peaceful streams. He renews my strength. He guides me along right paths, bringing honour to his name. Even when I walk through the darkest valley, I will not be afraid, for you are close beside me. Your rod and your staff protect and comfort me. You prepare a feast for me in the presence of my enemies. You honour me by anointing my head with oil. My cup overflows with blessings. Surely your goodness and unfailing love will pursue me all the days of my life, and I will live in the house of the LORD forever." (Psalm 23, NLT)

- How can you put the brakes on when you slip up?

- What ways could you stop a little slip up becoming a big slip up (next time)?

Stop and Reflect With Others

- How can others help you when you slip up?

- How has the last week been? Do you feel like you are on the right path? Why?

So Where Am I Now?

It had been raining all day, which is fairly typical for North-West England. All day I'd been running around, sending emails, having coffees, writing a talk, eating a whole packet of chocolate fingers for my lunch. But eventually the evening arrives, I'm not doing anything, and I'm home alone.

I can remember this situation from years ago. An evening home alone used to mean a green light for my testosterone to go into overdrive. No one's around, I can do whatever I want, and typically only one thing would of happen, and it wouldn't be watching Songs of Praise.

But this night, things have changed.

This time, I put on a film that wasn't X-rated, I ate pizza and then went to bed and went to sleep. Not once did I think about looking at porn. Not once did I have to resist everything in my body to try and keep myself from touching myself. Things really had changed.

Looking back now, it seems like a long time ago since I was trapped in a cycle of sexual sin. My life is anything but perfect. I still mess up. I still sometimes think about women in a way I shouldn't. But I feel immeasurably freer than I did all those years ago, over ten years ago now.

It wasn't easy to get to this point. It wasn't easy to change. I didn't find the whole process of living without sex on my mind 24/7 easy. It took me years. At some points I felt I was winning, and at some points I felt I was losing. But for the most part I now feel in control of myself, rather than feeling helpless and out of control.

I'm still in a fight. It's just that instead of me feeling like a helpless amateur fighting a boxing champion, it now feels like I'm the champion fighting an amateur.

— . — . — . —

God Was On My Side

Ultimately, the person that helped me through this was God. Without Him I would never have got to where I am today. I would never have escaped the cycle and applied the hand-brake and stopped if God wasn't in my life.

When I was trapped I questioned why God didn't just make it all go away. Why did I have all these feelings? Why did porn exist? Why did I have an uncontrollable penis? I wanted so much for God to just take it all away. I wanted to be free.

Surprisingly though, now I'm glad God didn't just click His fingers and make it all disappear. The journey God and I have been on since I hit puberty has been rocky. But that journey has shaped me and drawn me closer to God. My journey to freedom has had just as big an impact on my life as the actual freedom itself.

I didn't beat sexual sin on my own, God did it with me.

○ ○ ● ○ ● ○ ● ○ ● ○ ○ ● ○

Other People Were On My Side

Telling people about my problems, taking off my "holy mask" and being real with people, telling them that I looked at porn and couldn't really stop, was one of the most important steps towards freedom I ever took.

I used to think that telling people the mess in your life was a sign of weakness, that everyone else had everything sorted and you were the only messed up one. I now realise that telling people your mess is an immense sign of strength – it's easy for people to suffer in silence, but it takes real guts to speak out.

As I said before, I have a wonderful wife now too. She is both patient and forgiving. She tells it like it is (as anyone who knows her will tell you). As you know from reading this book, getting married is definitely not the answer and won't cure our problems for us, and isn't the 'prize we win' for being a good Christian. And the scars of my past can still haunt our life sometimes. But overcoming sexual sin became a possibility when I stopped seeing women as objects for my pleasure and started to respect them and see all women as children of God. It became possible for me to build a healthy romantic relationship, which lead to a strong marriage where sex is fulfilling. Where God's rhythm for my life and intimate relationship shaped everything.

Our fight really can lead us to a better place.

And honestly, sex isn't like the porn films, it's much better (after the first few months of working out how it works). Porn is fake, and only takes away meaning. But sex with the woman you have committed your whole life to, come rain or shine, is real, so it means something.

And I'm Still Fighting

I'm all too aware that I will have to fight the rest of my life to stay free from sexual sin. It's not a one off sell out title fight, but a daily fight. I hope to continue winning more than I lose. Not so I can write a book about how holy I am, but so I can closely follow my rescuer until I die.

You will make mistakes, you will mess up, but it's how you react that matters. For most of my life I didn't get up and fight again, I just sulked out of the ring feeling sorry for myself. But my hope and my identity is in God now, in His love and forgiveness rather than in my will power and determination. I have learnt to fight with Him alongside me, taking practical steps in my life, and through fighting I have found a freedom I would have given anything for ten years ago.

So I hope you can press the brakes, maybe slowly at first, but keep pressing them, stop, and find the life God wants to give you.

Helpful Resources To Help You In The Fight

Websites:

I recommend these websites highly. They have a mix of videos, blogs and testimonies, and all talk honestly about the issues surrounding pornography. Well worth a look:

- www.fightthenewdrug.org
- www.yourbrainonporn.com
- www.theporneffect.com

~~~~~~~~~~

Books:

If you want to read more, then these books will really help you out. The first one works best if you meet up with a mentor/someone you trust to discuss stuff with, but the others can be read at your own pace.

- *Refresh*, by Naked Truth Project
- *Every Young Man's Battle*, by Stephen Arterburn

Printed in Great Britain
by Amazon